YOUR KNOWLEDGE HAS VALUE

- We will publish your bachelor's and master's thesis, essays and papers

- Your own eBook and book - sold worldwide in all relevant shops

- Earn money with each sale

Upload your text at www.GRIN.com
and publish for free

Bibliographic information published by the German National Library:

The German National Library lists this publication in the National Bibliography; detailed bibliographic data are available on the Internet at http://dnb.dnb.de .

This book is copyright material and must not be copied, reproduced, transferred, distributed, leased, licensed or publicly performed or used in any way except as specifically permitted in writing by the publishers, as allowed under the terms and conditions under which it was purchased or as strictly permitted by applicable copyright law. Any unauthorized distribution or use of this text may be a direct infringement of the author s and publisher s rights and those responsible may be liable in law accordingly.

Imprint:

Copyright © 2017 GRIN Verlag, Open Publishing GmbH
Print and binding: Books on Demand GmbH, Norderstedt Germany
ISBN: 9783668613225

This book at GRIN:

https://www.grin.com/document/384391

Harry Mwololo

Use of SaaS (Software as a Service) as a Cloud Computing Solution

GRIN Publishing

GRIN - Your knowledge has value

Since its foundation in 1998, GRIN has specialized in publishing academic texts by students, college teachers and other academics as e-book and printed book. The website www.grin.com is an ideal platform for presenting term papers, final papers, scientific essays, dissertations and specialist books.

Visit us on the internet:

http://www.grin.com/

http://www.facebook.com/grincom

http://www.twitter.com/grin_com

Cloud Computing

Contents

Introduction

Customer satisfaction has been the key competitive strategy of Figura Leisure Centre. However, there is no clear information management system to help them achieve this. Doing the work manually is quite ineffective and time consuming. The organization is losing revenues because of poor management of data and communication system. There is no customer information and follow up on payments by staff is quite a challenge.

Proper communication among the staff is also missing. This makes it hard for the staff to respond to customer needs promptly and in the right manner. Customer feedback is also hard to get. Data processing, storage and communication are hard because, if done at all, it is through the conventional approach. This calls for the business to adopt cloud computing's Software as a Service system to enhance communication internally and advance interaction with external customers.

SaaS is quite suitable for small business and organizations like Figura Leisure Centre. With the use of SaaS there will be change in the way the organization conducts its business. When used appropriately, SaaS will decrease use of physical infrastructure, increased implementation speed, and recommendable client experience. SaaS will also save some upfront expenses (Rana, 2012). SaaS system would help the business in compiling customer information across various channels, and on point of contact between the organization and the customer.

Through CRM approach, the organization will be able to interact with clients through social media platforms. This will present an open forum for the organization members and clients to share experiences regarding the organization. Center management team will be in a position to organize and coordinate team conversations through an open channel that is dedicated to raise topic issues. Efficient sharing of documents and information within the business departments will be made easier. This will increase service delivery hence increased sales.

Cloud Computing vs. Conventional IT solutions

The key difference between cloud computing and conventional IT solutions is in the mode used in access or delivery of computing services coupled with the costs. Conventional IT solutions include the user having to share the remote server (Leading Edge, 2017). The cost of running a server is ever constant at all times even when the server is not utilized. Conventional IT solutions include having several hardware, like desktop, linked to a network through a remote server (Leading Edge, 2017). The server is normally installed on the resident premises, and offers every user access to the stored business data and apps (Leading Edge, 2017).

Characteristic of this mode is the additional hardware and software upgrades. Additionally, traditional IT solutions mode requires an additional IT department to be in place to handle the raising challenges (Leading Edge, 2017). Cloud computing comes out as a virtual hosting IT solution.

Cloud computing services are normally offered by cloud providers and normally charge for such services. Such services can easily be processed and availed with little management input (Leading Edge, 2017). Cloud computing offer users and business organizations various capacities to process and store their information in either a confidentially owned or data centers owned by third-parties (Rana, 2012).

Cloud computing include services like creating new applications and services, storing, backing up, and recovering lost data in a computer, website and blogs hosting, video and audio streaming, delivery of softwares on client's demand, and analysis of data for predictions and create patterns (Safari, 2004).

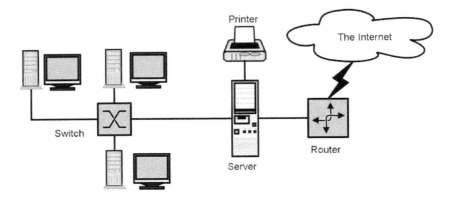

Fig. 1. Cloud Computing structure (Griffith, 2016).

Key Benefits of Cloud Computing

Cloud computing comes out as key shift from the conventional approaches of doing business using IT resources.

1. Cost

Cloud computing approach helps in eliminating the capital investment required in buying both software and hardware, establishing and operating data-centers for on-sites. It helps to do away with the serve racks, the round-the-clock electrical power for running and cooling the servers, IT personnel for running and managing the infrastructure.

2. Speed

A number of cloud computing services are offered on demand and self-service. This implies that a vast amounts of computing services and resources and be availed in a few minutes, usually with a few clicks of a mouse. This further provides the business organization with the desired flexibility and reduced pressure of capacity planning and resourcing (Rana, 2012).

3. Global Scaling

The merits associated with cloud computing include the capability of scaling elastically. In cloud speak, that implies the delivery of the right amount of resources is done in time.

4. Productivity

On-site data centers normally demand a lot of stacking and racking, software patching, hardware sets up, coupled with several other time-consuming IT operation and management obligations. Cloud computing helps to do away with the need for most of these requirements. This implies that the IT personnel can spend a lot of their time attaining more significant organizational goals rather than running IT resources (Rana, 2012).

5. Performance

The largest cloud computing services operate on a global network of fortified datacenters. Such data-centers are normally upgraded to the latest fashion of efficient and fast computing hardware. This provides various benefits over distinct corporate datacenter, including network latency reduction for apps and increased economies of scale (Rana, 2012).

6. Reliability

Cloud computing creates data backup, business continuity and disaster recovery cheaper and sassier. This is because data can easily be mirrored at several redundant sites on the network of the cloud provider.

Disadvantages of Clouding

Critics of cloud computing have argued that the cost of clouding is more as compared to the conventional solutions. They hold that it is less costly sending heavy packages through trucks than over the internet especially locally or within a region. The cost and speed of storing data locally outstrips the use of broad-area network ran by telecom firms. The telecoms, ISPs, and the media organizations control ones access (Safari, 2004).

Trusting the cloud implies that one trusts an unfettered, and continued access by externally. There is also the danger of crashing. Amazon, a cloud computing company that cloud stores data for big companies like Pinterest and Netflix experienced crashes in 2012. In 2014, companies like Dropbox, Basecamp, Gmail, Evernote, Adobe, and iCloud experienced such clashes. Microsoft, Google, and AOL had their share of the cloud clashes in 2015 (Rana, 2012).

Griffith (2016) claims that, with cloud computing, there is also the issue of intellectual property. The question of who owns the data that is store online, between the service provider and the user has been raised severally. In the past, there have been cases of controversy surrounding terms of service regarding data and information stored in the clouds.

Forms of Cloud Services: SaaS, IaaS and PaaS.

Cloud computing services come in three key kinds: platform as a service (PaaS), infrastructure as a service (IaaS), and software as service (SaaS). They are sometimes referred to as the cloud computing stack. This is because they are created on another's top. Understanding what these cloud services are and their differences make it easier to achieve business organization goals (Safari, 2004).

i). Infrastructure-as-a-Service (IaaS)

This is the most fundamental cloud computing service category. It is a prompt computing infrastructure, managed and provisioned over the internet. This serve swiftly gauges up and down with demand coupled with pay only for that one's use. IaaS assist one to avoid the cost and complexity of purchasing and running their physical servers and several other datacenters infrastructure (Safari, 2004).

ii). Platform as a Service (PaaS)

PaaS involves cloud computing services that make supply of on-demand environment for testing, developing, managing and delivering various software applications. PaaS is meant to create easier work for software developers to swiftly establish mobile and web based apps. This can be achieved by having worries about the set-up or running the underlying storage, servers, networks, and databases required for development (Rana, 2012).

iii). Software as a Service (SaaS)

Software as a service (SaaS) is an approach employed in delivery of software apps over the Internet, usually on a subscription and on demand basis. With SaaS, providers of cloud computing services can manage and host the software app as well as underlying infrastructure, while at the same time handling various maintenance services such as software upgrades, and patching of security. Several users are linked to the app over the Internet, normally with the help of web browser on their computers or mobile phones, or even tablets. Common SaaS services examples include calendaring, email services, as well as office tools such as Microsoft Office 365 (Safari, 2004).

Advantages of SaaS over the others

One Advantage of SaaS is that it offers a full software solution that one can buy on a pay-as-you-go approach from a provider of a cloud service. An organization can rent an app's use and its users link up with it over the Internet, normally with a web browser (Safari, 2004). All of the underlying infrastructure, app software, middleware, and app data are situated in the data center of the service provider. The provider of the service runs the software as well as the hardware (Rana, 2012).

With the right service contract, the service provider can see to it that the security and availability of the app and the user's data are well provided. SaaS lets the organization to move quickly and operate with an app at reduced upfront cost (Safari, 2004). SaaS makes complex enterprise apps such as CRM, and ERP pocket friendly to even small business organizations that do not have the financial muscle to deploy, purchase and the needed software and infrastructure (Angeles, 2017). The user pays only for what they make use of. This further, helps the user to save money since SaaS automatically scales up and down depending on usage level (Rana, 2012).

Use of Free Client Software

Users get the chance of running the SaaS right from their web browser without downloading and installing the software, though some softwares demand plugins (Safari, 2004).

Easy to Mobilize Workforce

With SaaS, it becomes easy to mobilize workforce since users have access to SaaS data and apps from any mobile or PC with Internet. There is no need to develop new apps or run them in a different computer. This is because the service provider does all these for the user. Additionally, there is no need for hiring special expertise to run matters security. A good service provider ensures that the data security is there (Safari, 2004).

Data can be accessed from anywhere. Users are able to access their data or information from any computer or devise as long as they are connected to the Internet.

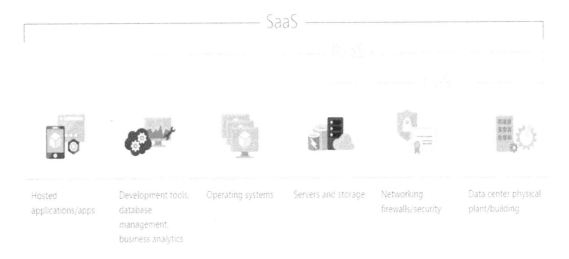

Fig 2. SaaS, PaaS, and IaaS services (Microsoft, 2017).

Rival Competitors in the Industry

Cloud computing has transformed the information technology industry. Since it creates good income, it has attracted stiff competition from the major service providers who are all in the race to claim the lead. Consequently, the industry has become hyper competitive in some innovative and new ways. The top four competitors in the cloud computing industry include Amazon, RackSpace, Google and Microsoft Azure (Rana, 2012).

Amazon is the king of this jungle, with its Elastic Compute Cloud (EC2) services. They are known for their attractive services to the business groups. Amazon is also known for their friendly approach towards customers. Currently, the EC2 is running on a whopping 450,000 servers. It is also the most preferred business organization for cloud computing because of S3, its simple storage service provisions (Rana, 2012).

RackSpace comes out as the main competitor after Amazon. It is a leader in cloud web hosting and involves managed hosting services. It comes out as number two in terms of revenue and virtual machines. It has public cloud service revenue of $189 million in 2011.

Google takes the third position with its Google App Engine platform. It is perceived as one of the few business organizations which possess the potential to capitalize in essential computing firepower. Its cloud service is targeting development and hosting web based apps with the use Google data centers, and infrastructure. It has added merit in that the search engine supports various languages like Ruby, Java, and Python.

Microsoft is thriving in the cloud commerce with its Windows Azure Platform. This platform is only two years old but it is causing ripples in the attractive industry. Azure is really giving the key competitors a run for their money. Azure offers software developers with an option of hosting, developing and running web based apps. It offers a full set of services such as computing environment, database functionality, scalable storage and a content delivery network (Rana, 2012).

Adopting Salesforce.com as a SaaS based CRM for FLC

Customer Relationship Management (CRM) involves the practices, technologies and strategies used by organizations to run and analyze client interactions and organization data throughout the customer lifecycle. This is done with the aim of improving business relations with the customers. It also assists in customers' retention and increasing sales for the business organization (Xin, 2015). Salesforce.com has been one of the leading cloud based CRM systems in setting the bar higher. It integrates CRM to mobile then to social Medias. It helps the organization to track sales opportunities and changes in the market.

Benefits of Salesforce.com to FLC

The system will help in compiling customer information across various channels as well as on point of contact between the organization and the customer. These could include the organization's phone numbers, mails, social media interactions, live chat, and conventional marketing materials. It also offers customer's personal info, their purchasing history, concerns as well as buying preferences (Xin, 2015).

Through CRM approach, the organization will be able to interact with clients through social media platforms like Twitter, Facebook and LinkedIn. This will present an open forum for the organization members and clients to share experiences regarding the organization. Center management team will be in a position to organize and coordinate team conversations through an open channel that is dedicated to raise issues (Feng, 2013). The app will also limit more sensitive interactions to private and invite-only conversations.

The team members will also be able to intact directly through secure and private direct messages (Feng, 2013). Center management committee will be able to share files, spreadsheets, PDFs, and office documents with ease. They will also have the option of including comments and highlighting some issues for future references. All notifications, files and messages are automatically archived and index (Feng, 2013).

Challenges of adopting Salesforce.com

Data security will be a key concern for Center as far as the use of SaaS based CRM is concerned. The organization will not have direct control over the maintenance and storage of the data (Xin, 2015). In case the cloud service goes out of business or another company acquires it, the data can be compromised. There is also the challenge of clashing of the cloud data. Center might also experience the challenge of cost in terms of subscription for softwares may be higher than conventional approach (Xin, 2015).

To overcome the issue of cost, the company will only pay for the software only when it will be using, therefore, in the long run the cost would be lower. In cade of data security the company and have contract with the service provider that the data will be secured even if the company enters into different contract with another company. Clashing of data happens for a few hours. This will not hinter the business from running effectively.

References

Angeles, S. (2017). Best CRM Software 2017. *Business News Daily*. Retrieved April 04, 2017 from, http://www.businessnewsdaily.com/7839-best-crm-software.html

Griffith, E. (2016). What Is Cloud Computing? Retrieved April 04, 2017 from, http://www.pcmag.com/article2/0,2817,2372163,00.asp

Feng L, (2013). Cloud computing adoption by SMEs in the north east of England: A multi-perspective framework, *Journal of Enterprise Information Management*, Vol. 26 Issue: 3, 250-275,

Leading Edge. (2017). How is Cloud Computing Different from Traditional IT Infrastructure? Retrieved April 04, 2017 from, https://www.leadingedgetech.co.uk/it-services/it-consultancy-services/cloud-computing/how-is-cloud-computing-different-from-traditional-it-infrastructure/

Microsoft Azure. (2017). What is cloud computing? *A beginner's guide*. Retrieved April 04, 2017 from, https://azure.microsoft.com/en-in/overview/what-is-cloud-computing/

Olawale, D. (2014). *Crucial Differences between Cloud Computing and Conventional Computing*. Retrieved April 04, 2017 from, http://techatlast.com/cloud-vs-conventional-computing/

Rana, N. (2012). The Unified Theory Of Acceptance And Use Of Technology (UTAUT): a literature review. *Journal of Enterprise Information Management*. 35(6), 443 - 488

Safari, F. (2004). The adoption of software-as-a-service (SaaS): ranking the determinants. *Journal of Enterprise Information Management*. 28(3), 358-378

Xin, T. (2015). User acceptance of SaaS-based collaboration tools: a case of Google Docs. *Journal of Enterprise Information Management*. 57(7), 423 – 442.

YOUR KNOWLEDGE HAS VALUE

- We will publish your bachelor's and master's thesis, essays and papers

- Your own eBook and book - sold worldwide in all relevant shops

- Earn money with each sale

Upload your text at www.GRIN.com
and publish for free

www.ingramcontent.com/pod-product-compliance
Lightning Source LLC
LaVergne TN
LVHW080120070326
832902LV00015B/2695